Opposed Marketing

How To Double Your Business In 3 Months By Doing The Opposite Of Everybody Else

Mitchell Miller

Copyright © 2014 Opposed Media Inc.

All rights reserved.

www.opposedmedia.com

ISBN: 1500322148
ISBN-13: 978-1500322144

Reprinting, teaching, or in anyway ripping off the information included herein, is in violation of copyright law, subject to civil and criminal penalties, and is just not cool at all. Credit to other sources has been given credit where credit is due.

Disclaimer: All opinions, ideas, and strategies I talk about in this book are for educational purposes only. Everything written in this book is true, proven, and works. But it may not work for you. I do not know your work ethic, background, personal situation, learning disability, or how you interpret what I write. Most people have a hard time listening to directions properly. All I present here is logic, reason, and examples of actual people who have used these strategies to build their businesses.

"I am told by people all the time that they simply do not have time to read and listen to all the material they have purchased or subscribed to.

But time is democratic and just. Everyone has the same amount. When I choose to read with my mid morning coffee break and you choose to blather about trivia with friends, when I choose to study for an hour sitting on my backyard deck at day's end but you choose to watch a TIVO'd American Idol episode, we reveal much.

When someone says he does not have the time to apply himself to acquiring the know-how required to create sufficient value for his stated desires, he is a farmer surrounded by ripe fruit and vegetables, whole grains, and a herd of cattle on his own property who dies of starvation, unable to organize his time and discipline himself to eat."

- Dan Kennedy

CONTENTS

	Acknowledgments	i
ii	Introduction	1
1	It's All About Positioning	Pg 5
2	The Power Of Direct Response	Pg 11
3	What Is Your Marketing Budget?	Pg 17
4	Guarantees	Pg 19
5	Raise Your Prices	Pg 22
6	Important Questions	Pg 25
7	Conclusion	Pg 29

WARNING

Before you devalue, or disregard these ideas and information, know that not a single day goes by where I, or my friends do not receive an email, or letter telling of how applying these strategies have helped them make more money. These are PROVEN marketing systems that have, and continue to generate millions of dollars to those who apply them. There is no good reason you will not get comparable results. You must open your mind to change, and test these ideas out.

INTRODUCTION

I am very fortunate these days to have more consulting clients than I have time for coming to me "pre-sold" mostly by referral. I am woefully out of practice at convincing people of the value of my advice. I do understand however, that my business revolves around other industries, and so you have most likely never heard of me. Given my schedule, I don't have much time to give you my entire history (You can easily find it online). I am going to give you the short and sweet out of necessity.

You may be tempted to argue or reject what I say in this book. I'm ok with that, it's your choice. A lot of what is in this book will contradict what you have been told or what you think is right. You must understand that you will be successful to the extent that you are willing to break and defy industry norms. If you do what everyone else does, you will have the same results. Every item of advice I give within these pages is tested, proven, and experience based.

I value my time HIGHLY, and so I value yours as well. I will not waste your time by regurgitating feel good phrases, or bullshit theory that has no practical use in real life. I'm also not concerned *why* something works. Only that it does, and to use it to make more money. EVERY piece of advice I will give you is also transferable to any other business, product, or service.

People are routinely paying me $10,800 a day to sit down and discuss their marketing situations with them personally. All too often we spend too much of that day laying the groundwork. So let this be a primer. I hope you find this book provocative and valuable.

"Whenever you find yourself on the side of the majority, it is time to pause and reflect."

- Mark Twain

ITS ALL ABOUT POSITIONING

In order to make the big marketing shift in your business, we have to get back down to basics, and agree on a few things.

First, we must understand that business can be defined as selling products or services to a marketplace. These products and services must be valuable to the people buying them. So you can say that business sells value. What determines value, and how valuable a product or service is?

The law of supply and demand.

Stick with me here. If you offer a service, and there is more supply of you than there is demand of you, does your value go up or down in the perception of your market? Of course down. Now what happens when there is more demand for you than there is a supply of you? Does your value go up or down? The first big shift you need to make is that you MUST get the law of supply and demand working in your favor. Let me explain.

Failing to engineer the law of supply and demand in your favor, is the sole reason you are chasing business, selling yourself, and convincing people to work with you. It is also the reason there is any price resistance with your customers. As we will talk about in the pricing chapter, the more you use the law of supply and demand in your favor, the more you can charge any price you like.

Once you change this, everything changes. Everything becomes easy. Are you a pest, or a welcomed guest? If you look at the way that 99% of businesses advertise and market, you will notice they are doing what we call "push marketing". Here's what I got, look how cool we are, buy my shit.

It is equivalent to a boy chasing a girl. Yes she may be interested in someone like you, but telling her how cool your car is doesn't work. Similarly your business is the same. Your customers do not care how great you are. They care only about what you can do for them. So forget the cute slogans, or witty advertising.

To make the second huge shift in your marketing strategy, you need to understand that you do not want to do what the majority does. Avoid it at all costs. If you do what everyone else does, you will have the same results as the majority. And the majority gets mediocre results. If you want better results, do the opposite of what everyone else is doing. This alone, without changing anything else you do will differentiate you. Literally. Stop chasing business. You must flip the script. Just like romance, whoever chases holds all the power.

We call this Push marketing vs pull marketing. Are you going after business, or is it going after you. This is something you must engineer from the start. Even when the reality is you are not in that position. In the business world, once you have a reputation, once you are known for something, it is difficult to change.

So it's a little like the chicken and the egg. You must go about manufacturing extreme demand for yourself. You must manufacture demand and limit your supply. Immediately.

The reality will catch up to what you have created because perception is reality. But you must begin to make the switch. This is not deception, this is understanding the basic laws of business and human psychology. You must also understand that the very best in the world are doing this at a high level all the time. Everything you see on the news, the celebrities, it's all an illusion. It's all manufactured, it's all perception. This is the game, embrace it. If you have this, then everything I will teach you, you can use in an ethical trustworthy way. It's up to you.

The first thing to do in your business to achieve this is to do education based marketing. People will buy from who they learn about it from. It's who they now trust. Want a simple strategy you can use right now to step in this direction?

Create a consumer awareness guide for your market.

Use lead generation advertising to give it away (next chapter). Then collect emails and mailing addresses. **There is no greater, and more important business function than building a database of interested potential customers, and current/past customers.** Nothing.

You are going to have to get damn good at writing and be

prolific. Or have someone else write for you .

Write articles, put out videos. These pieces of media can answer objections the customer may have. Write a book.

You must achieve expert authority status (Dare I say celebrity status) within your market. Align with respected people in your market or town. An aura borrowed is almost as good as an aura owned. That means you are as important as the people you are seen with.

There is also barely any difference between false media and true media in the eyes of your market. An article written about you in the wall street journal only has a little more power than an article written about you in the wall street select, a blog you created just for this purpose. People don't see the difference or care. It is important to write about yourself in the form of press releases, articles, and books.

If you are a freelancer or a one man service, Have an intake procedure to handle new customers. Make them jump through hoops to get to you, this is important. Don't answer your phone. What successful person do you know who you can get to on the first try? Busy in demand people are busy.

There is also a practical benefit to having an intake procedure like this. You are managing expectations in advance so you don't break them when you get too big. If you are always known as the guy who they can easily reach, well what happens when you do grow? You can't possibly meet that expectation, not if you are successful. You now have pissed off customers because you created a standard you couldn't possibly keep up with. Ryan air is known for having extremely terrible flying conditions. They also have one of thew lowest rates of customer complaints. Why? Because they set it up in advance.

Understand that ordinary acts become extraordinary acts only because you set them up in advance. So if you know that no matter how big your company gets, you can always answer the phone within 48 hours, then it may be of great benefit to you for people to know that you are so busy it usually takes 5 business days to respond. So now, when you do respond in 48 hours, it becomes extraordinary. People are impressed. Whatever you do be careful not to setup customer expectations that you cant meet as you grow. It's hard to change your reputation.

This chapter gave you an overview of what we call positioning. That is, positioning yourself in your market as the most in demand, highest priced, most knowledgeable, hard to get business man or woman. We all know how seductive hard to get is. We want what we can't have, and we value that which is difficult to obtain. People love it. So give them what they want, make your self hard to get. It will make your life so much easier. Follow me, because in the next chapter I am going to show you exactly how to structure your advertising so that you have a a constant flood of leads and customers coming in everyday. From here on in, I am going to give you actionable make money immediately strategies.

Lets go.

"You are surrounded by simple, obvious solutions that can dramatically increase your income, power, influence and success. The problem is, you just don't see them."

- Jay Abraham

THE POWER OF DIRECT RESPONSE

To keep life simple and not overwhelm you, I am going to give you a specific advertising strategy you can go apply in your business right now. This will be unlike all the advertising you have ever done before. Why? Because you are going to learn the power of direct response lead generating advertising. Once you learn and apply this type of advertising, you will be opened up to en entire world of this type of advertising.

Lead generation is opposite of what most people do. Most likely you run an advertisement, giving the customer only one reason to do business with you right now. Come into the store and buy. Go to this website and buy. Think of car dealership commercials. The typical commercial says come on down today and check out our employee pricing sale. $10,000 off, and we are giving away balloons and puppies. Dan Kennedy calls this "a bridge too far". It's too much to ask. You are only speaking to the people who are on the verge of buying, or ready to buy today. There is a big problem with this type of message: It leaves out 95% of your market.

Your ad doesn't cater to all the other people who are not ready to buy yet but who are still interested in the product. A bridge to far.. but sometime in the next month, 2 months, or 6 months, they are going be ready. So you spend all this money on advertising to try to sell right off the bat. All those people who aren't yet in a position to purchase right now (which is 95%+) won't and can't respond. YOU JUST ALIENATED 95% OF YOUR MARKET. It's like putting out a personals ad saying how awesome you are, and that you need to come meet me today. And get married. Without knowing me. Without a relationship. This is a selfish and inefficient way of advertising, yet you all do it.

Lead generation offers a consumers guide or some sort of free gift relevant to their pre purchase questions. You capture the contact information of that 95% group of people, and put them into a database and relationship with you in advance. You now get the chance to work on them.

Do you see how you can literally get nearly ALL the customers in your market, and how your competition will be left with the scraps because they are not doing this?

So by talking to them, being with them, building their trust until they are ready to buy, and educating them along the way... you ensure that they and their friends buy from you. So it's a very easy switch to make. Instead of advertising to the few% that will buy now, you are advertising to everyone who is generally interested. AND YOU GET THE ORIGINAL 5% WHO WOULD HAVE BOUGHT FROM YOU ANYWAY.

You now get two harvests from the exact same ad dollar. If

you do this right, expect that eventually half will purchase from you. This doesn't include referrals, and referrals of referrals etc.. This one shift alone will more than double your business. This works in any business or industry. Here is an example. Think how this can apply to your business.

Imagine you are a magician. You put an ad in the paper that says

"Magician For Hire. I do parties, holiday events, and corporate events. Great prices, great service. Order now and get 10% off".

It is safe to say that is the same type of advertisement that you or anyone else would usually run. Maybe add a cute slogan or something.

People like gotta be like pretty much ready to hire a magician right then and there. Odds are they aren't gonna cut out the ad and keep it. They'll lose it. If you did lead generation advertising that offers a free report instead, you'd have immediate sales and a big bank of leads to follow up with. A big list to draw money from. Forever. Your ad could be as simple as:

"Warning: Do not hire a magician for your party until you read this FREE REPORT titled: 6 Deadly mistakes people make when hiring a magician, and how you can make sure you choose the right magician. Visit www.magicianservice.com/freereport right now."

Every lead generating ad you put out grows your list. You could even do partnerships with a photographer or all sorts of parallel but not competitive businesses. All this **in addition** to the regular business he would have got with the old ad.

You can then qualify those people that are ready to do business now, and more importantly disqualify those who do not meet your standard as a client you want to take. So there is an efficiency benefit here. Focusing your time and resources on those who you want to deal with. You can then funnel those disqualified leads to a competitor for a price.

So if you understand we are doing two things now, we need something to entice those people to begin a relationship with us. We call this a lead magnet. Something of enough value to those people that they would pay for this information but you give it to them for free. Free recorded message, free report, free book.

Pay attention to the market and what media they will prefer their lead magnet. Do not rely on digital only, as huge % of population is not online. As well, a physical product still has more perceived value. Also you have no logical reason to justify getting full contact information if it's only digital. And you want their full contact info to make your ROI the highest. As well, the higher up the age ladder, the more offline you want to go. If you are only marketing to people under 60, you are only trying to eat 30% of the economic pie. Not too smart.

We call this low threshold vs high threshold. You need to get in the mindset of baby stepping your market into doing business with you.

A bridge too far is dangerous and wasteful. A financial planner that runs a newspaper ad offering prospective clients to see a free presentation is too much. Your asking them to read a small newspaper ad, then get in their car to come to your office (they don't know you), and go to a presentation where they know they are gonna be pitched.. very high threshold. Only the people ready to purchase very quickly something are gonna do that.

On the other hand, if you took all that away. Don't talk workshop, presentation, product, service, or appointment. Just a lead magnet. Unbranded. *"Warning - don't even think about hiring a financial planner until you know the 7 questions you must ask any financial planner.... pick up your free report here etc.."*

These types of ads are not mutually exclusive. You can still run the same type of ads you have been as well. Or even add a lead magnet to the bottom of one of your traditional ads. If you must. I believe it is useless to do anything other than lead generation. Image advertising is far too expensive, and costs far too much money to be of any real, measurable effectiveness. Let them get to know you in a vacuum. On your list. Sales happens in a vacuum. One on one, with you and your client.

I hope you grasped the power of direct response, making them respond from the ad so that you can measure and track your return on investment. Because if you are running traditional advertising, you have zero way to track exactly how much you made vs. how much you spent on that particular campaign. In my mind that is wasteful, in efficient, stupid, and lazy. You must be able to know how well you did. Lead generation allows you to not only do that, but also scoop up 95% of the pie your competitors wont.

"Budgets are important"

- Some idiot

WHATS YOUR MARKETING BUDGET?

This is going to be a short chapter. The concept of a marketing budget pisses me off. Many of my consulting clients have this limiting belief that there ought to be a set number of dollars you allocate to marketing and advertising. Let me explain to you as quick as I can that having a pre-set marketing budget is the stupidest thing you can ever do.

There is this belief that there is a finite amount of money to split in the business, and if you subtract some from one area, another area will suffer etc... This thinking is wrong, and very damaging to your business. If your philosophy about money includes budgets, let me liberate you right now. You are about to make a lot more money.

So, you develop a budget for the year. In advance for the coming year. We'll what's wrong with that picture? Well It's a predetermined restriction on how much your sales can be for the entire year based upon a formulaic equation against your sales.

When really your advertising budget should be to spend as much as you possibly can, as fast as you can turn the money over so you can sell more, advertise more, turn that money over to sell more, advertise more..

Who knows how much you should spend on advertising this year, because you don't know how the hell much you are going to be selling this year yet. So you are grossly limiting and capping how much your business will grow for the coming year. You may have to re read that over. I know I did when I first figured it out.

So what do you do instead? You have an allowable cost per sale or per lead or per transaction. "I'll spend up to 100 per sale, or per lead or whatever, and you can bring me all the people you can"

GUARANTEES

In any transaction, one side is always asked to assume most or all of the risk. As a business, the more we can shoulder that risk, the more the customer will buy. Jay Abraham calls this risk reversal. You want to reverse the risk for the customer. Most companies guarantee their product or service anyway. I mean you are gonna make it right for them if they aren't happy, so you might as well bring that guarantee up to the front and scream it out loud. Most people wont do that, but it is extremely powerful.

Offer a free trial wherever you can. Let them try out your product or service. Offer a no questions asked lifetime guarantee. By bringing it to the front, and pretty much begging them to return it if they aren't 100% satisfied, your sales will skyrocket. You will find that your refund rate doesn't even move.

That being said, I have discovered something very cool about guarantees. The higher caliber of client you have, or higher priced the product or service you offer, the less important having one is.

This goes against what we would naturally think. Counter intuitive. Billy Bob is buying something for $200 for which $200 is a significant amount of cash for him, you pretty much have to have a guarantee. Give him the best one you got.

You have to in some way, reverse the risk for him.

A guy spending $2000 for which $2000 is or isn't significant money for him, a guarantee is less necessary. Someone spending $20,000? you virtually don't even need a guarantee at all.

What's going on here.

Well to even be in the position to give you $20,000 of his money, a significant amount to him or not, he has kind of gotten past the idea of needing the reassurance.

For example, take business conferences. At a $200 conference, you better have all sorts of drinks, food, and everything short of a 3 ring circus in order for then to feel good about being there. Fancy booklets, a nice pen to take home.

Someone paying $2,000 you can get away with like coffee and juice.

At $20,000 you can just give them water, and tell em to sit on the floor. They are there for different reasons than the $200 herd.

So higher the price tag, and stronger the relationship you have with a client, will determine how extreme of a guarantee you use.

My general rule is the lower price, lean on them. Use them to justify the entire sale. At higher prices it's like an "oh by the way" kind of thing.

At the higher price points where you know you aren't going to need a guarantee, it can be cool to use an anti guarantee. You can briefly harp on the fact that you do not believe in a guarantee.

Also, don't guarantee where you don't need to. This can come from not fully believing in your skills and abilities, and is a form of self sabotage. Also don't guarantee where any of the result relies on the customer having to maintain what you did for them. 8 out of 10 times they will screw it all up anyway.

So use this knowledge to save time and aggravation in your business. Trust me, this works. I guarantee it.

"My preaching on this has been consistent for over 20 years: if you can't be THE cheapest, there's no benefit in being almost the cheapest. What kind of ad slogan is that? No sane single guy goes into a busy bar at Friday happy hour, climbs on a stool and loudly proclaims he's the 5th best lover there. If you're in a commodity business –get out. I mean: reinvent."

- Dan Kennedy

RAISE YOUR PRICES

You are about to discover closely guarded secrets of businesses that regularly charge 5-10 times more for their products and services than their competitors.

Price is the path to unlocking hidden value, overlooked opportunities, and even business freedom for you as an owner. It involves creatively repositioning your business so it can be perceived differently than other businesses. This way, customers line up begging to do business with you; rather than viewing you as just another "pizza place". Raising your prices is one of the only ways to dramatically increase your profits without doing much. After all, if you doubled your prices and made no other change, you have effectively just doubled your business.

One of the worst mistakes you can ever make is to automatically assume that "everyone" buys based solely on price. That couldn't be further from the truth.

If that were the case why doesn't everyone only go to Earls, or Moxie's instead of Ruth Chris, or Gordon Ramsey's Steakhouse where steaks can be 5 – 10x more expensive? And why do you see people lined up at 5 am to buy the latest iPad when there are comparable tablets by dozens of companies for much less. The bottom line is only 10% of consumers make their buying decisions based on price. If this were not the case everybody would be staying at super 8, dressing at Wal-Mart, and drinking no name cola.

So what does this have to do with your business? If you are failing to extract the maximum price your market will pay for your goods and services, then you are leaving money on the table and out of your wallet. This is a simple fact that is robbing you of money, time, and freedom. Less time with family and friends, and less time to screw off and do fun things. All the things you thought you would be able to do when you initially started the business.

Another thing: You should never, EVER be the low cost provider in your industry. Why?

You simply can not keep it. There will always be some dummy who will come in and offer the same thing at a lower price, which in turn will drive your prices down, and thin out your wallet even more. Even if they lose money doing it, they will stick around long enough to be a huge problem for you. So never try to be the low cost provider, you cant sustain it. If you can't be the absolute cheapest, there is no value or benefit in being almost the cheapest. "Hey girls, I am the 5th best guy in this room, wanna go on a date!". My main point is that you can pick your level of clientele. Find another basis other than price to compete on.

A lot of businesses pay way too much attention to industry norms. They look at what other businesses are charging, the high and the low, and price somewhere in between. Most selling occurs in a vacuum with you and your customer, and the marketplace will pay you what you ask of it. Re read that last sentence if you need to. Very powerful insights.

Here are a few pricing tips. Raise your prices as high as you can. Do it in increments, and test the results. If you raise your prices 20%, and notice almost no customer drop off, then you raise them again. Keep raising, and keep testing. How do you know when you have reached the maximum price your market is willing to pay? As an example, if you own a restaurant and you are full every Friday evening, raise your prices. Raise them until the customer count begins to drop. I have seen restaurants double their prices over very short periods of time without a drop in reservations.

Work on your price presentation. How you say it is almost more important than what you say.

There is a reason Wal-Mart charges $19.95 instead of $20 for certain items. Test, test, test. Test different offers, different payment structures, have sales, discounts, special event pricing, and turn products and services into monthly subscriptions.

Remember, if your market is willing to pay more for your products and services than you are currently charging, you are doing them no benefit or service. You are only short changing yourself by imposing your beliefs and opinions on the marketplace instead of listening to your market and adhering to the basic laws of supply and demand.

Raise your prices today. Your customers wont mind.

IMPORTANT QUESTIONS

You now have a context to how I like to market, and the incredible power that you now have. Here are a few questions to ask yourself, and concepts to think about.

1. USP

Why should I choose you over your competitors? This is your hook, or gimmick. You MUST answer this question to stay in business for any length of time. You need to justify your own existence in the marketplace. Great service doesn't cut it. Listen to the question again: What do you do or offer that none of your competitors do, that will make your customers want to do business with you over them?

"30 minutes of its free"

"Overnight delivery, guaranteed"

This is your positioning. It's all tied together with the first chapter.

2. LTV

So the first question I ask a client is what about your business differentiates you from your competitors? We just covered that.

Next I ask how much you are spending on marketing and sales? How did you arrive at that number? What's the LTV of an average customer?

The LTV is the lifetime value of a customer. Think about this. Until you actually know what a customer is worth to you in total dollars, how could you ever make a proper decision on how much you can afford to spend to acquire one?

This is how to calculate what a client is worth to you:

What is the average customer worth to you in gross dollars:

Unit of sale
Frequency
Yearly frequency

For example. Your average customer spends $80 the first time, buys 4 times per year at $120, is with you an average of 2 years, and refers 5 people in those 2 years.

The average business owner only sees the customer as an $80 sale, maybe some more money down the road. But what are the real numbers?

80 + (120 x 4) x 2 = $1040. Add in the 5 referrals, and each

customer on average is worth $6,240 over the lifetime in your business. If you average 100 new customers in your business per year, you are growing by $624,000 for ever 100 customers you acquire. So if a customer is worth over $6,000 and 5 referrals, are you really going to piss and moan about spending $50, or even $1,000 to acquire him?

In business, he who can spend the most to get a customer wins. This can be a battle of who has the deepest pockets, who can take that loss and finance themselves until the back end starts paying out.

This doesn't even put into consideration all the marketing strategies I talked about and will talk about in this book to increase sales. This can get exponential!

This allows you to pay sales people more, and then they are 10x more motivated to go and make sales for you because you can give them more of the initial sale.

3. Questions to ask your business:

Where is your business coming from?

- new
- repeat

You may find you are not spending enough time on those channels that bring in the most business for you. 80/20

Who stands to benefit more than you for you being more successful?

You could be 80% of a suppliers business. They may be apt to fund, to help, to support you. working out a referral program, advancing capital, time, sales people, Co op advertising, barter

Who is in the position and already spent considerable capital, time, and energy to having goodwill, and would be open to endorsing, strategically aligning, and other wise do some sort of partnership where you can work in parallel without stepping on each others feet, and share customers

Is there any way to add hard to soft or soft to hard in order to build value to your customers?

Examples:

Adding hard to soft: Free movie coupon with lawn cut.
Adding soft to hard: Free training with purchase of our phone

4. Don't re invent the wheel

Call up the most non geographical competitors, and say " hi I'm Mitch Miller. I run a successful landscaping company in Canada. Now I just want you to know that I never plan to do business in The USA, and if you plan on doing business in Canada you might not want to take this call. But I think it would be advantageous for us to build a relationship where I share what's working well for me, and vice versa. A mastermind where we can help each other with advice."

CONCLUSION

I could write 20 more books on these type of concepts. However, Let this book serve as an introduction to a world of marketing you may not have seen before. My goal with this first book is to just get you to make the switch. From being a push marketer to a pull marketer. There are literally an endless amount of strategies and tactics to implement in your business, and I believe you are capable of making big leaps in your business starting toady. If you would like help in carrying out these strategies, I do consult with business owners. As of this writing there is a waiting list, and you can hunt me down and put yourself on it if you like. I must warn you in advance that I charge very high fees, and am not easy to work with. But If you can get to me, it will be well worth it to you. I hope one day to have the honor of helping you make more money in your business.

ABOUT THE AUTHOR

Opposed media is a consulting, marketing, promotion, and publishing company that was established by Mitchell Miller to solve an underlying problem in the advertising and marketing field: the lack of measurable results.

Mitchell Miller is available for one on one phone consulting/coaching to select entrepreneurs starting at $2500/hour, or $10,800 for the day. There is currently a waiting list, and he does not work with corporate clients. Mitchell travels and has had clients in Canada, USA, Western Europe, and northern Africa in a variety of industries including luxury villa rentals, landscaping, wedding planning, restaurants, nightclubs, and cooking schools. He has appeared in the November 2010 edition of Fast Company magazine, and for the last 2 years operated a landscaping business. Mitch is a published author, and musician. He was the bass player for the band The Casanova Playboys, which had achieved nationwide Canadian radio play. Mitch and lifetime friend Jamie Salloum recently formed a new band called The Stars Fell, and are currently recording the hit album "Night Night", out for release in 2015.

Printed in Great Britain
by Amazon